TEEN LIFE™

FREQUENTLY ASKED QUESTIONS ABOUT

STDs

Nicholas Collins
and
Samuel G. Woods

ROSEN
PUBLISHING®

New York

Published in 2012 by The Rosen Publishing Group, Inc.
29 East 21st Street, New York, NY 10010

Library of Congress Cataloging-in-Publication Data

Collins, Nicholas.
Frequently asked questions about STDs / Nicholas Collins, Samuel G. Woods. 2-12
   p. cm.—(FAQ: teen life)
Includes bibliographical references and index.
ISBN 978-1-4488-4630-6 (library binding)
1. Sexually transmitted diseases—Juvenile literature. 2. Sexually transmitted diseases—Miscellanea. I. Woods, Samuel G. II. Title.
RC200.25.C65 2012
616.95'1—dc22

                          2011000303

Manufactured in the United States of America

CPSIA Compliance Information: Batch #S11YA: For further information, contact Rosen Publishing, New York, New York, at 1-800-237-9932.

Contents

WHAT ARE STDS?

STDs are sexually transmitted diseases, or diseases spread through sexual intercourse. According to the Centers for Disease Control and Prevention (CDC) as of 2009, there were roughly nineteen million new STD infections each year. Nearly half of those cases occurred among people aged fifteen to twenty-four. The cost to the U.S. health care system is believed to be as much as $15.9 billion per year. STDs are a major public health concern.

STDs may be widespread, but they are rarely talked about. There is a stigma, or a mark of shame, attached to them. Some people feel ashamed and embarrassed that they have contracted a disease through sexual activity. This is one possible reason why many people do not visit the doctor as soon as they suspect that they have been infected.

Over the last four decades, there has been a considerable effort made to reduce the spread of STDs. Although the rate

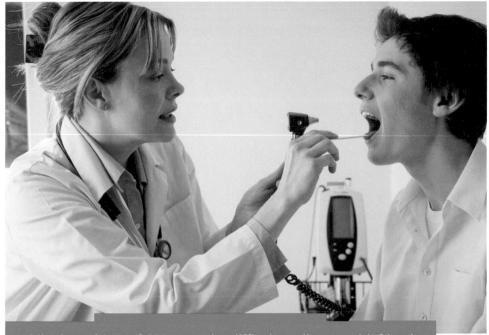

While the subject of STDs may be difficult to discuss with friends, family, and even doctors, it's important that you get tested if you suspect that you might be infected.

of infection in America has been brought to an all-time low, it is still the highest rate in the industrialized world. The rate that STDs spread among teenagers is difficult to control. In the most extreme cases, one person could spread the disease to thousands of others within a matter of weeks. Some people are not even aware that they are carrying a disease as they spread it to others. If you think you might have symptoms of an STD, and you have been sexually active, you should seek immediate treatment.

Women in particular suffer if they do not see a doctor immediately. An STD left untreated can cause serious problems in the body, such as infertility and pelvic inflammatory disease (PID), which affects the female reproductive system. If a baby is born to a mother who has certain STDs, the baby can be blind, suffer from mental retardation, or have bone deformities. Fortunately, today's medicines can cure many STDs and ease the symptoms of others. But if you do not see a doctor, you risk severe consequences. Education is vital for helping those who are infected and reducing the spread of STDs. It is important that everyone practice safe sex so that the incredibly high rates of infection can be reduced.

How can you recognize the early signs of an STD? Where can you go for treatment? What are the best ways to protect yourself from these diseases? This book will give you the facts. We will talk about sex and how your body works. We will discuss safer sex methods and other issues to consider if you have sex. You will learn that there is no reason to be ashamed of an STD. Millions of people live with STDs. You are not alone. There are people and places that can help you, and certain STDs are curable. But it is important to get all the facts: the worst danger that you face is ignorance.

Though each STD is unique, all STDs share certain similarities. They are all transmitted through sex or intimate body contact, and they are all dangerous if they are not treated. Some can cause slow and painful death. Many STDs have similar symptoms. But some STDs have no symptoms at all. Common symptoms of STDs may include discharge from the penis or vagina; redness or itching of the genitals; pain or burning during sex or during urination; and sores, blisters, or bumps in the genital area. One thing is true for all STDs: they must be treated as quickly as possible.

The Causes of STDs

Like all diseases, STDs are caused by different kinds of germs. A germ is a microscopic invader of the body. Germs get into the body in many different ways. Most diseases are caused by two types of germs: bacteria and viruses. Bacteria are tiny organisms that live in the body, plants, water, and air. Not all bacteria are harmful, but some bacteria cause disease. Bacteria, for instance, cause food poisoning.

Viruses are other tiny agents of infection. When a virus gets into the body's cells, it stops the cells from performing their normal jobs. When you feel sick, the symptoms you feel are caused by your body's reaction to the invading virus. The common cold and the flu are viral diseases.

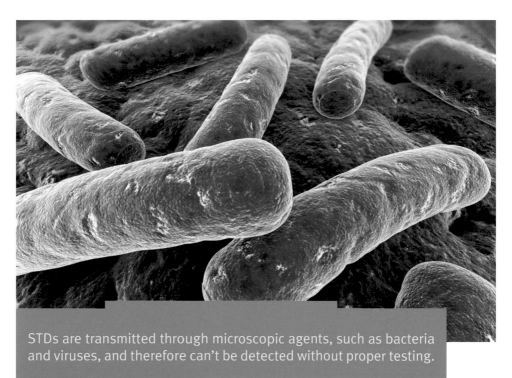

STDs are transmitted through microscopic agents, such as bacteria and viruses, and therefore can't be detected without proper testing.

Sexually transmitted diseases are contagious diseases. This means that you can catch them from another person. Unlike a cold or the flu, which are also contagious, sexually transmitted diseases are not spread through coughing or sneezing. STDs are caught only by intimate sexual contact with a person who has the disease.

Contagious diseases are serious and scary. They can spread very fast. One person can spread the disease to hundreds or thousands of other people. Here is an example: One infected person has sex with ten people. Then each of those people has sex with ten other people. That means that 101 people have been exposed to the disease. What if each of those people has sex with ten people? Then 1,010 people have been exposed. And all because of one infected person.

Most STD infections occur in sexually active teenagers. The more partners that you have, the more you increase your chances of contracting a disease.

How Do We Prevent STDs?

You have probably heard people say that safe sex can protect you from getting a sexually transmitted disease. The only truly safe sex is no sex. But if you decide to have sex, the best way to prevent STDs is to follow responsible sexual behavior. That is why using a condom is smart. Condoms (also called rubbers) are latex casings that are slipped over an erect penis before sex. They prevent direct genital contact between partners. Without direct genital contact, the chance of contracting a disease or

While condoms and other forms of protection may decrease the risk of spreading STDs, they aren't a guarantee. The only surefire means of protection is abstinence.

giving someone a disease is much smaller. Condoms are also a very effective form of birth control.

Other birth control methods, such as diaphragms used with spermicidal foam, partially protect women from some STDs. They can also protect men from some diseases. These methods are not foolproof, though, and should always be used together with a latex condom. The birth control pill does not prevent STDs at all. Safe sex also means knowing about your partner's past sexual behavior—and being honest about your own history. This is important because your partner's previous sexual partners have an effect on your health. We will discuss other ways to practice safe sex in the next chapter.

How STDs Are Spread

STDs are a major health problem in the United States today, especially among teens. There are approximately twenty different sexually transmitted diseases out there. Many of these diseases cause pain and discomfort. They can also be expensive to treat and can have long-term and sometimes dangerous effects.

One reason that teenagers are at particular risk is because their immune systems are not fully developed. In addition, teenage years are a time of experimentation. Some teens try drugs and alcohol as they establish their identities. Under the influence of drugs or alcohol, teens are more inclined to take risks. They are also less likely to use adequate protection to prevent or reduce the likelihood of getting an STD.

Teens and young adults make up a large part of the number of Americans infected with STDs. According to the CDC in 2009, 51 percent of new STD cases consist of people between the ages of fifteen and twenty-four. Young people are particularly at risk because they are more likely to be single and engage in risky behaviors than are older adults, according to the report.

Although the total number of people with STDs has been rising in recent years, many people are learning methods of prevention. As more and more people learn the facts about preventing STDs, the growth rate of infection may slow down in the future.

Often one partner will blame the other for giving him or her an STD. This attitude is unfair. When two people have sex, they are both responsible for what happens. If a person knows, however, that he or she has an STD, it is only fair that he or she tell any sex partners about the STD. STDs are always a serious matter.

The Most Dangerous STD

The most frightening STD is AIDS, or acquired immunodeficiency syndrome. As of 2010, according to the CDC, there were an estimated one million Americans infected with HIV (the virus that causes AIDS), with roughly one in five of those unaware that they were infected. It is a serious problem. Many people have lost family members or friends to this deadly disease. We hear about movie stars and sport stars such as Magic Johnson being affected by HIV and AIDS in the news. Much has been done to educate the public about AIDS, which includes talking to teens about the disease and explaining the importance of safe sex.

Although it is the most dangerous STD, AIDS is not the only STD. Many young people are infected with one or more STDs, such as syphilis, gonorrhea, genital herpes, genital warts, chlamydia, and trichomoniasis.

HOW DO STDS
AFFECT THE BODY?

STDs are transmitted through sexual contact, and usually the sex organs are the first to show signs of an STD. A good way to learn how to prevent STDs is to know how your body works and how your partner's body works.

The male sex organs are located both outside and inside the body. The penis and the testicles (or testes) are outside. The testes are in a sac called the scrotum. They produce sperm, which are contained in a liquid called semen. At sexual climax, the penis releases the semen in a series of muscular spasms called ejaculation.

When semen enters a woman's vagina during sexual intercourse, it can travel to the woman's fallopian tubes, fertilize an egg (if present), and make the woman pregnant. In most cases, men with an STD carry the bacteria or virus in the tube inside the penis. The disease is then passed through the penis with the semen.

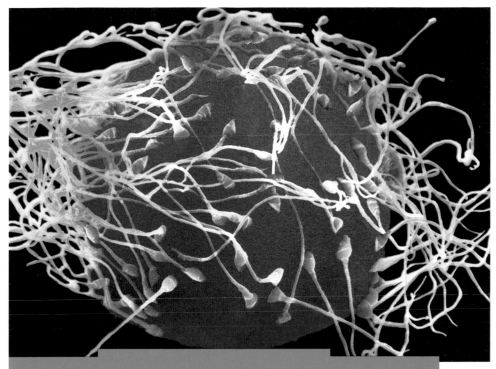

One way STDs can be passed along is when a man's semen fertilizes a woman's egg. Many different types of disease can be transmitted through semen.

The external female sex organs together are called the vulva. The vulva consists of the labia (vaginal lips) and the clitoris. The clitoris, which is located in front of the vagina, becomes stimulated during sexual activity. Most of a woman's sexual organs are inside her body. The vagina is the passage that leads to the uterus (womb). The fallopian tubes extend from either side of the uterus. There is an ovary at the end of each tube.

Each month, one of the ovaries produces a mature egg cell. The egg is then released from the ovary and into a fallopian tube. When the egg is in the tube, it may be fertilized (impregnated) by a sperm. If the egg is fertilized, it will attach itself to the wall of the uterus and begin to grow. If it is not fertilized, the egg will be flushed out of the body through menstruation (the menstrual period). To prevent STDs, it is important to know that when a woman is sexually excited, her labia and vagina become moist. Bacteria can easily grow and multiply in this warm, moist environment. When the woman is touched or penetrated by her partner's tongue or penis, these bacteria can be exchanged.

Intimate Contact

Intimate sexual contact means an exchange of bodily fluids—saliva, semen or vaginal secretions, and sometimes blood—that occurs during sexual relations. When you kiss or penetrate your partner's genitals, any germs or viruses present in these fluids are exchanged between you both.

Kissing on the mouth also exchanges a bodily fluid called saliva. But kissing usually is not very dangerous. The exception to this rule is if one person has an outbreak of herpes. A cold sore can transmit the herpes virus to another person (this will be explained in more detail later). Kissing may also be dangerous if one person has an STD infection in his or her mouth or throat.

The only guaranteed way to prevent contracting a sexually transmitted disease is to not have sex. There are many ways to express your affection that do not involve sexual intercourse. Cuddling, massaging, kissing, and touching are all safe.

There are many ways STDs can be transmitted through intimate contact. There are also many safe ways to have intimate contact that are safe, such as hugging and cuddling.

If you decide to have sex, then do it safely. Make it a habit to use condoms. Condoms greatly reduce the chance of contracting or giving someone a sexually transmitted disease, and they greatly reduce the chance of pregnancy. But condoms do their job only if you use them properly.

Condoms can be bought in many places. Since AIDS has become a serious health problem worldwide, condoms are more widely available. In addition to being sold in any drugstore, condoms can often be found in school health clinics, Planned Parenthood offices, doctors' offices, gas stations, and public restrooms.

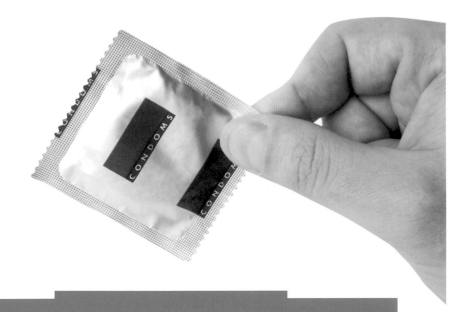

While abstinence is the only guaranteed way to prevent the spread of STDs, contraception should always be used during intercourse.

Some people do not want to bother with using condoms. A condom must be put on an erect penis, or one that is stimulated. For some people, this means stopping at a bad time. But a condom may keep you from contracting HIV and other STDs, and it may prevent pregnancy.

Condoms

Never use a condom with an open wrapper. Put the condom on before the penis touches the vagina, mouth, or anus. Hold the condom by the tip to squeeze out air. Leave some space at the tip to hold the semen. Unroll the condom all the way over the erect penis. If you feel the condom break or slip off, stop immediately and put on a new one. After sex, the man should hold the condom at the rim and pull his penis out slowly while it is still hard. Use a new condom if you have sex again. Here are some tips to keep in mind: Not all condoms are the same. The most effective condoms are made of latex. Condoms made of plastics should also be highly effective.

Condoms made of lambskin or other natural material are more porous and do not protect against STDs. If you use a lubricant to make penetration easier, choose one made with water (such as K-Y Jelly). Never use skin lotions, baby oil, Vaseline, or cold cream with latex condoms. The oil in these products weakens the condom, and it may break. Always treat condoms gently. Most important, use a condom every time you have intercourse—oral, vaginal, or anal. Use a new condom each time.

Protection from STDs is the responsibility of both partners in a sexual relationship. This means that although you have the right to expect your partner to do his or her part, you must also be prepared to do your part.

Keeping condoms nearby is smart. It does not mean that you are easy. It also does not mean that you must have sex. It only means that if you decide to do it, you will be able to protect your health. Remember, do not carry condoms in your wallet if you carry your wallet in your pocket; your body heat will disintegrate the condom.

The female condom, a new and effective way of preventing both pregnancy and STDs, is a polyurethane (plastic) pouch that fits inside a woman's vagina. On each end of the pouch is a soft ring. The outer ring stays on the outside of the vagina and partially covers the labia. The inner ring fits inside the vagina, like a diaphragm, to hold the condom in place.

The female condom is convenient because it can be inserted up to two hours before sex—you do not have to do it on the spot. If you have sex again, though, you need to use a new condom.

Some Things to Know

Two things can be used to protect you during oral sex. For oral sex on a man, you can use condoms—many are made especially for this purpose (some condoms are even flavored). For oral sex on a woman, it is best to use a dental dam. This is a piece of latex that fits over the woman's vagina and labia, preventing an exchange of fluids.

If you are aware of the following things, you can greatly reduce your risk of contracting an STD. If you are already infected, you can increase your chances of detecting it early. STDs can spread very easily. Sexual intercourse with someone who has had sex with many other people in a short period of time is a risk. Each person that your partner has had sex with increases the chances that he or she has a disease, which increases your chances of getting it. A relationship with only one uninfected partner is safer.

Look carefully at your body. Know what your body looks like normally. Pay attention to how you feel as well as how you look. Keep an eye out for any changes in your body. Pay attention to these changes. Ask yourself how long they have been there. Are they going away or are they getting worse? Could these changes be caused by something else, or could they be signs of an STD?

Watch for any changes in appearance or any other problems. Do not be afraid or embarrassed to question your partner about his or her body. It could save your life.

Myths and Facts

 If you don't have any signs or symptoms of an STD, you must not be infected. Fact: ➥ Many STDs don't have obvious symptoms. Some people don't know they are infected. This is why it is so important to get tested.

 Engaging in only oral or anal sex, but not vaginal intercourse, is a way to prevent catching an STD. Fact: ➥ Many STDs, including gonorrhea, can infect areas of the body such as the throat, anus, or rectum. The delicate tissues of the rectum can actually make it more vulnerable to infection.

 You have to have multiple sexual partners to catch an STD. Fact: ➥ Anyone who is sexually active is at risk of being infected, even if he or she has sex with only one person or has had sex just once. The risk of getting an STD can be greatly reduced by always using protection and by talking about your sexual history with your partner before you decide to become sexually active.

three

HOW DO I PROTECT MYSELF AGAINST HIV AND AIDS?

You have probably heard a lot about AIDS, but you may not think it has much to do with you. When AIDS first hit the news, people thought that only homosexual men or drug users could get the disease. But we now know that anyone can get it.

AIDS stands for acquired immunodeficiency syndrome, a disease in which the body's immune system is weakened. Normally, the immune system fights off infections and diseases. When the system breaks down, a person can develop a variety of life-threatening illnesses. Eventually the person can die from one or a combination of these illnesses.

AIDS is caused by a virus called human immunodeficiency virus, or HIV. When a person is infected with HIV,

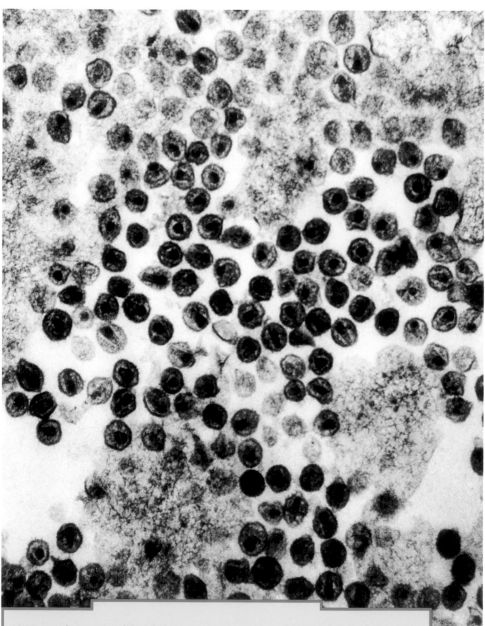

HIV, as shown in this electron micrograph, is the virus that causes AIDS. There is still no cure for AIDS, and it continues to be one of the most dangerous STDs in existence.

he or she is said to be HIV-positive. Once the human immuno-deficiency virus is inside the body, it begins to grow and multiply. Then it attacks the body's immune system.

Normally, when a virus or germ enters the body, the immune system immediately begins to fight the invader. White blood cells try to kill the cells of the body that have been invaded by the virus.

The white blood cells try to stop the virus from multiplying and spreading to more cells. If the white blood cells cannot kill enough of the virus cells, the virus will take over, and the person will be vulnerable to infections. Once infected, it's difficult to bring the person back to health.

Doctors do not know everything about how the immune system is destroyed by HIV. And they do not know how to stop HIV from multiplying. They do know, however, that once the human immunodeficiency virus has started to do its work, the body will soon lose its ability to fight disease.

Once the immune system is destroyed, the person cannot fight off even the most common viruses and germs. When the person's white blood cells have diminished to a certain point, the person is said to have AIDS.

HIV is not AIDS. It is possible to be HIV-positive for many years and not have AIDS. But about half of the people who are infected with HIV will eventually get AIDS within ten years. The exact length of time it takes to develop AIDS, and the severity of the AIDS-related illness or illnesses, will differ from person to person. Many factors play a part, including the person's overall health.

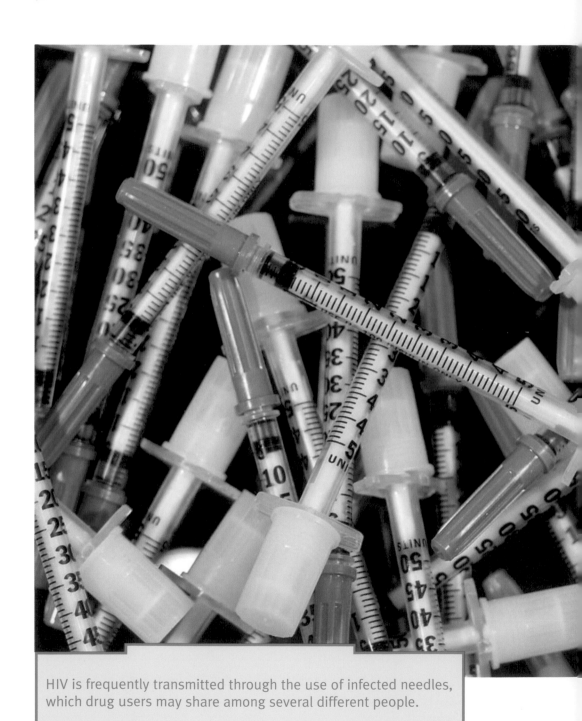

HIV is frequently transmitted through the use of infected needles, which drug users may share among several different people.

How HIV Infects the Body

There are two main ways to become infected with HIV: having unprotected sexual intercourse with an infected person (this can be vaginal, oral, or anal sex) or sharing drug needles or syringes with an infected person. Also, women infected with HIV can pass the virus to their babies during pregnancy or while giving birth. Blood transfusions have transmitted the disease as well. However, since 1985, all blood donations have been carefully screened, so this type of transmission is less likely.

You can be infected with HIV and have no symptoms at all. You may feel perfectly healthy, but if you are infected, you can pass the virus to anyone with whom you have unprotected sex or share needles or syringes. Many infected people have no symptoms and have not been tested. If you have unprotected sex with one of them, you put yourself in danger.

The Symptoms of AIDS

AIDS has many symptoms. Often, they take a while to appear. People can carry HIV for a number of years and still look healthy. Patients may have some or all of the symptoms. Each body's immune system resists AIDS in a different way. The most common symptoms are:

- Extreme weakness and fatigue
- Swollen lymph glands
- Rapid weight loss
- Stubborn cough
- Coated tongue and throat
- Easy bruising and unexplained bleeding
- Frequent fever
- Night sweats
- Bumps, rashes, tumors, or other strange developments on the skin
- Trouble recovering from common illnesses such as a cold or the flu

Stopping the Disease

In the last ten years there has been considerable research into finding a cure for HIV and AIDS. Scientists are closer to understanding the virus and finding a vaccine for it. Drugs have been developed to slow down the spread of HIV in the body, making life for people with HIV a little more manageable until a cure can be found.

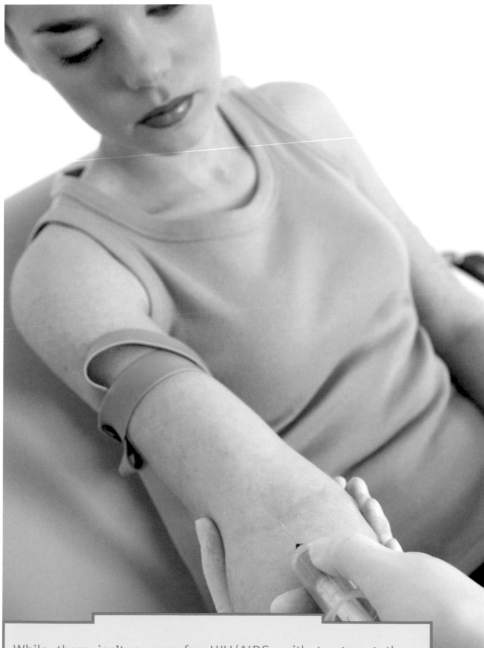

While there isn't a cure for HIV/AIDS, with treatment those infected can expect to live full lives. However, they still need regular testing and doses of medication.

You may think AIDS cannot happen to you. But it can. The best way to reduce your risk of becoming infected with HIV is to not have sex. If you decide to have sex, your best protection against HIV and other STDs is to use a latex condom. Also, you should find out as much about your partner's sexual history as you can.

Another way to protect against HIV is not to share needles or syringes if you use illegal drugs. (You should not use illegal drugs at all, but that is a different discussion.) When getting your ears or other body parts pierced, or when you are getting a tattoo, go to a qualified person who uses sterile equipment.

The HIV-antibody blood test determines if the HIV virus is in your blood. The test is confidential. It is now possible to take the test by mail, but you may prefer to take the test at a doctor's office or clinic. It is important to talk with a qualified health professional both before and after the test is done.

Myths About Contagion

While there are many ways you can transmit an STD, there are just as many myths about contagion. Therefore, it's important to be able to distinguish the facts from the rumors. According to the CDC, you cannot catch HIV from:

- Donating blood at a blood bank
- Everyday casual contact with infected people at school, work, home, or anywhere else
- Clothes, drinking fountains, phones, or toilet seats

- Eating food prepared by an infected person or sharing cups or other eating utensils
- Mosquito bites, bedbugs, lice, flies, or other insects
- Contact with sweat, saliva, or tears

You also cannot get HIV just from kissing someone. Although it is possible to give or get HIV through deep or prolonged kissing, especially if you have a cut or sore in your mouth or throat, most scientists agree that this is not a common way for the virus to be exchanged.

Ten Great Questions to Ask Your Doctor

1 What kind of tests should I have to screen for STDs?

2 Which is more effective for STD prevention, the male or female condom?

3 What should be done if the condom breaks during intercourse without our knowledge or slips off?

4 Once I'm cured of a particular STD, is it possible to get that STD again?

5 How can I prevent getting an STD again?

6 Will using condoms with spermicide that contains nonoxynol-9 lower my chances of HIV infection? Do any spermicides help lower the risk of infection from HIV and other STDs?

7 Can you tell that someone has an STD just by looking at him or her?

8 Do my parents have to find out if I have an STD?

9 I've had unprotected sex. Should I get an HIV test? How long after I had unprotected sex should I get the test? How long will it take to get results?

10 How can I talk to my partner about my STD?

WHAT ARE SYPHILIS, GONORRHEA, CHLAMYDIA, AND TRICHOMONIASIS?

According to the CDC in 2009, a total of 13,997 cases of primary and secondary syphilis were reported. Syphilis is caused by a tiny germ called a spirochete (SPY-ruh-keet). Spirochetes are bacteria. They are very, very small and can live almost anywhere in the body. Syphilis is also contagious. It is a venereal disease, which means it is transmitted only through sexual contact. Syphilis has a rather long incubation period. That means it takes a long time for it to grow and become noticeable. The incubation period for syphilis is three weeks to three months.

After incubation, a sore appears at the site of the infected area. The sore is infectious for as long as it can

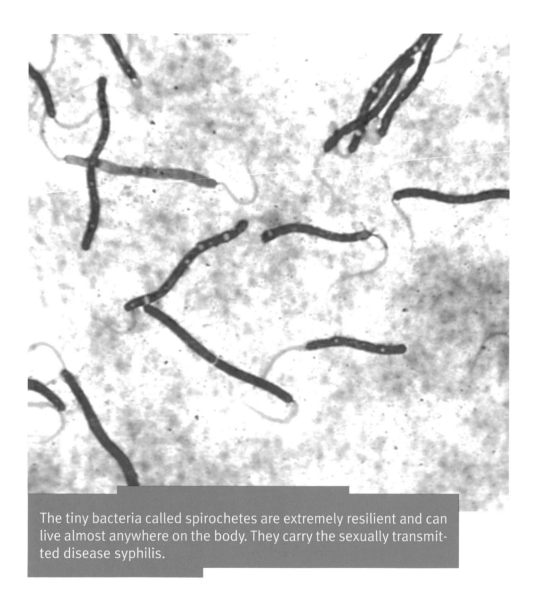

The tiny bacteria called spirochetes are extremely resilient and can live almost anywhere on the body. They carry the sexually transmitted disease syphilis.

be seen. The spirochetes are in the sore. The spirochetes carry the disease.

A syphilis sore is called a chancre (SHANG-ker). A chancre can look like a cut or rash. A person can become infected with syphilis by having direct contact with an open sore. The sore may be in the mouth, vagina, or rectum, or on the penis of an infected person. During sex, the man's penis comes in contact with the vagina, rectum, or mouth of his partner. These are usually the organs that have the syphilis sores. That is when the spirochetes move into the body of the healthy person.

The Stages of Syphilis

A chancre sore will develop on the part of the body where the infection was passed. This is called the primary lesion of

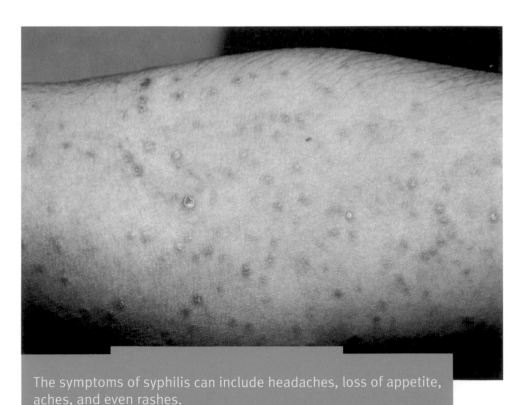

The symptoms of syphilis can include headaches, loss of appetite, aches, and even rashes.

syphilis. Usually this sore will look terrible. It may look red, and it may be wet. But this sore does not usually cause pain. It is just very unsightly. Sometimes the primary sore is easier to see. It may be on the penis. But many syphilis sores are not easy to see. They can be inside the vagina or under the foreskin of the penis or under the tongue or inside the rectum. Often the infected person does not see the sore. After a few weeks the chancre disappears. When a chancre heals, there is a feeling of relief—the infected person feels as if the syphilis has "gone away." But it has not gone away. It is just hiding inside the body until later.

If the sore has disappeared and the syphilis is still not treated, the disease gets more serious. It enters the secondary stage. The secondary stage is anywhere from six weeks to six months after the infection began.

In the secondary stage, the spirochetes have multiplied throughout the whole body and symptoms can take different forms. Most symptoms develop in the mucous membranes and the skin. The mucous membranes are the soft linings inside the body cavities, like the nose and mouth. A rash can break out on the skin anywhere on the body. It often appears on the palms of the hands and the soles of the feet. Patches of hair can fall out, too.

When these symptoms appear, it means the person is very contagious. A partner will get syphilis from the person. The symptoms can last for weeks. Eventually they go away. But even when they go away, the syphilis stays.

After the second stage disappears, the person has latent syphilis. Latent means hidden. A person with latent syphilis may no longer have any symptoms, but a blood test would still show the disease. Most people are not infectious after they have had syphilis for one year. But if syphilis is left untreated for long, it can cause brain damage. Spirochetes can destroy brain tissue as well as affect the heart, skin, and bones. There are other symptoms of untreated syphilis. Spinal cord damage and paralysis can occur. Many victims lose their ability to walk and see. These are results of the spirochetes slowly damaging organ tissue.

It is very dangerous for a pregnant woman to have syphilis. A pregnant woman will pass the disease to her baby during childbirth. Syphilis in newborn infants can cause deformities and even death. Treating syphilis is simple, especially if begun early. It can be treated and cured by penicillin. If a patient is allergic to penicillin, the doctor can give another antibiotic.

Gonorrhea

According to the CDC, 301,174 cases of gonorrhea were reported in the United States in 2009, an 11 percent decrease from the previous year.

Gonorrhea is caused by the bacteria *Neisseria gonorrhea*. These bacteria cannot live outside the human body. They live in the mucous membranes inside the eyelids, mouth, rectum, penis, or vagina. It is not true that you can get gonorrhea by casual contact. You cannot get it from a doorknob or a toilet seat. You cannot get it from a handshake or through a cut in the skin. The only ways for it to pass from one person to another are through sexual activity and childbirth.

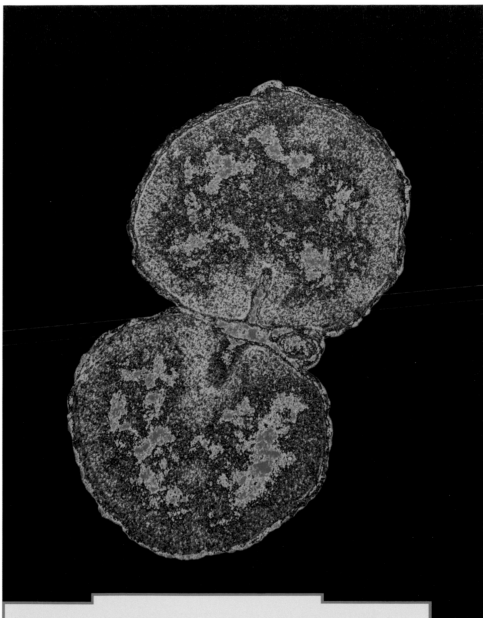

Neisseria gonorrhea are the bacteria that cause the sexually transmitted disease gonorrhea. They can live in a variety of places on the body where mucous membranes are present.

When a healthy man has sex with a partner who has gonorrhea, the bacteria enter the parts of the body with mucous membranes that are used during sex—the penis, mouth, or rectum. Gonorrhea commonly enters the urethra, the tube in the penis that carries the man's sperm and his urine to the opening at the head of the penis. In the urethra, the bacteria start to multiply.

Every ten to fifteen minutes they double in number. Within hours there are millions. This incubation period can last up to twenty-eight days, but the usual period is one to ten days. The body tries to fight the infection, but the white blood cells are quickly outnumbered. The dead white blood cells and the bacteria form pus, which collects in the infected area. After incubation, symptoms begin to appear. There is usually a burning feeling when urinating. Pus oozes from the penis. This is when most people realize that something is wrong and go to the doctor or clinic. It is better, however, to treat gonorrhea before these symptoms appear. Otherwise it can be even more serious.

Bacteria will travel from the urethra to the testicles. Pus in these organs can leave scar tissue. The scar tissue can cause a man to become sterile. That means he is unable to have children. Untreated gonorrhea can also cause arthritis and heart trouble.

A man is just as likely to have gonorrhea as is a woman. A man can give gonorrhea to a woman during sex, and a woman can give it to a man. When people are infected, chances are they will infect a partner during sex.

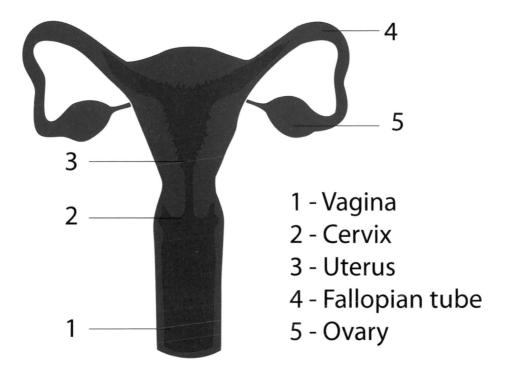

1 - Vagina
2 - Cervix
3 - Uterus
4 - Fallopian tube
5 - Ovary

Gonorrhea can be transmitted through a woman's sexual organs. This diagram illustrates the areas where the bacteria enter, settle, and thrive.

When a healthy woman has sex with a partner who has gonorrhea, the bacteria enter through the parts of the body with mucous membranes used during sex. Most often the bacteria enter through the vagina. When they enter through the vagina, the bacteria stay in the cells of the cervix at the opening of the uterus.

Sometimes the infection causes a mild burning sensation during urination. Sometimes pus will discharge from the vagina, but it is most common for it to be asymptomatic (no symptoms are seen).

When the bacteria travel to the other sex organs, the infection is more serious. The bacteria will settle in the uterus and/or fallopian tubes. When these organs are infected, pus builds up and causes swelling and pain. There can also be fever and pain in the abdomen. If gonorrhea is left untreated, the woman may eventually become sterile.

If a pregnant woman becomes infected with gonorrhea and is not cured, the baby can pick up the bacteria during birth. Most likely, the infection will get into the baby's eyes and cause blindness.

Treating Gonorrhea

Gonorrhea bacteria can be detected under a microscope. A pus sample will show the bacteria. Doctors treat gonorrhea with antibiotics. In many states, gonorrhea is no longer treated with penicillin. That is because some kinds of bacteria are not killed by penicillin. Patients in these states are treated with another medication that can kill the bacteria.

Chlamydia

Until recently, chlamydia was considered the fastest-spreading STD in the United States. It is especially common among teenagers and young adults. According to the CDC, 1,244,180 cases of chlamydia were reported in 2009.

Chlamydia is caused by the bacteria *Chlamydia trachomatis*. Like other STDs, it is transmitted by direct contact with the genitals, rectum, or mouth during sex. The tricky thing about identifying a chlamydia infection is that most infected women and up to one-half of infected men have no symptoms. Chlamydia symptoms may show up within a week after exposure but usually take up to a month to appear.

Because chlamydia often affects women's internal reproductive organs, some women experience pain during sexual intercourse, a pain in their lower abdomen, or bleeding between menstrual periods. Otherwise, the symptoms of chlamydia are similar to those of gonorrhea. Both women and men may experience a low-grade fever or a burning sensation when urinating. Discharge from the vagina or penis is also a common symptom. Men with chlamydia may also feel a burning and itching around the penis, and sometimes the testicles become swollen.

Because chlamydia is so difficult to detect, doctors advise people who are sexually active to be tested for the STD once a year, even if they feel healthy. If you find out that you have chlamydia, tell your sex partners right away. Your partners should also be tested, even if they have no symptoms.

If chlamydia is not treated, it can cause serious health problems. In fact, it is the leading cause of infertility, especially among women. Fortunately, the infection can be treated and cured with antibiotics. By getting treatment quickly, you can prevent lasting damage to your reproductive system.

Once the symptoms of trichomoniasis appear, it's important to see a doctor fairly quickly. He or she can prescribe antibiotics.

Understanding Trichomoniasis

Another STD that is difficult to detect is trichomoniasis, or "trich." Trichomoniasis (trih-kah-mah-NY-ah-sis) is most widely known as a women's disease because it can cause vaginitis, an irritation of the vagina. But men can get it, too. Because most men and many women show no signs of the disease, it is easy for one couple to pass trich back and forth between them.

Trichomoniasis is caused by a parasite that grows on the sex organs. Trich is spread mainly by sexual intercourse, both heterosexual and homosexual. Unlike other STDs, however, the parasite that causes trich can survive for a few hours not only in vaginal fluid, semen, or urine, but also on damp towels, washcloths, or bedding. Trich can also be spread by mutual masturbation if fluids from one partner's genitals are passed to the other. As with other STDs, a latex condom should stop the infection from spreading.

When symptoms of trich do occur, they appear within four to twenty days after exposure to the disease. But it is also possible for signs of trich to show up years after infection. In women, symptoms can include a heavy yellow-green or gray vaginal discharge, pain in the lower stomach, discomfort during sex, itchiness around the vagina, painful urination, or an urge to urinate more often than usual. Women may have spotty bleeding in their vaginal discharge.

It is common for men not to show symptoms of trich. Men with trich may have a whitish discharge from the penis and painful or difficult urination. And most men recover from trichomoniasis without treatment within a few weeks. But because it is likely for a man with trich to spread the infection to his sex partners, it is a good idea to get checked by a doctor if you do have any symptoms. A doctor can prescribe antibiotics that will cure the infection. This medicine should be taken by both partners, or you might find yourselves passing the infection back and forth.

Besides causing vaginitis, trichomoniasis is not a great threat to your health. But it often occurs along with other STDs, such as gonorrhea. Because of this, if you have trich, ask your doctor to check you for other infections.

GENITAL HERPES: WHAT ARE THE FACTS?

You probably have heard of herpes, but you may not know a lot about it. Herpes is caused by a virus called herpes simplex. The virus causes sores on or near the mouth or on the genitals. It can also infect the eyes by contact with a finger that is contaminated. Once a person gets herpes, he or she may have outbreaks of sores for the rest of his or her life. When an outbreak happens, the person can spread herpes to others.

Herpes in Greek means "to creep." The virus was given this name because it can hide in the body for a long time without being detected. Then, without warning, it can come out and cause trouble. There are eight kinds of herpes, and all are caused by viruses. Not all herpes viruses are sexually transmitted. One causes chicken pox and shingles in adults, another causes mononucleosis ("mono"), and still another causes

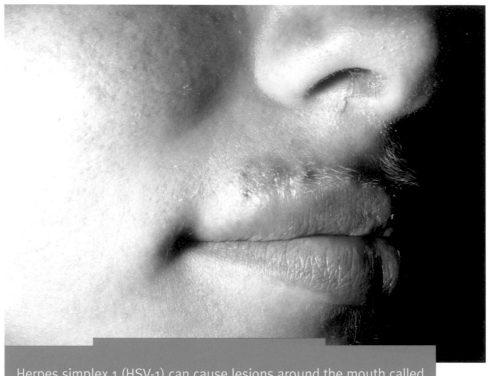

Herpes simplex 1 (HSV-1) can cause lesions around the mouth called cold sores. The STD can be transmitted through infected saliva.

cytomegalovirus (CMV). Herpes simplex 1 (HSV-1) causes cold sores and blisters, usually on the mouth, and herpes simplex 2 (HSV-2) causes genital herpes. Both HSV-1 and HSV-2 can be sexually transmitted.

The Spread of Herpes Simplex

Both oral and genital herpes are spread only through direct skin-to-skin contact. You cannot catch herpes just from sitting next to an infected person. But you can get it if you touch them in a place where they are infected.

Unlike some other STDs, you can get herpes just from kissing someone who has a herpes cold sore. If you have a cold sore on your mouth and have oral sex, you can give your partner herpes simplex 1 on his or her genital area. If you have active genital herpes (even if you have no symptoms) and you have vaginal or anal intercourse, you can transfer the virus to your partner during sex.

Genital herpes is usually contagious only at certain times. Because symptoms are sometimes barely noticeable, herpes is often spread by people who do not even know that they are infected. Using a latex condom every time you have sex can prevent you and your partner from sharing herpes. Contraceptive foams or jellies that contain the spermicide nonoxynol-9 have been proved to help stop the spread of the herpes simplex virus. Always use the spermicide together with a condom.

One difference between herpes and other STDs is that you can reinfect yourself with herpes. If you touch a herpes sore, you risk moving the virus to other places on your body. This is most likely to happen during the first outbreak of herpes. The solution: Don't touch. If you do, wash your hands as soon as possible. The herpes virus is killed easily with soap and water.

Symptoms and Treatment

After you have come into contact with the virus, symptoms of herpes usually develop within two to twenty days. The symptoms are usually the worst when you are first infected. The sores may burn, itch, or tingle. If the sore is in the urethra, you might feel a burning sensation when you urinate. You may get a headache, fever, muscle aches, or swollen glands. You may also have a poor appetite, and you may feel tired.

After the first outbreak, herpes seems to disappear. But it is only hiding. Once the herpes virus is in the body, it is there for life. From time to time, the virus is reactivated. When that happens, it travels back down the nerves to the surface of the skin, and another outbreak of herpes occurs. Usually the new outbreak happens near the spot where the first infection happened.

For some people, herpes comes back often. Others have outbreaks only once in a while. (The average is about four recurrences per year.) Even though all outbreaks are uncomfortable, the symptoms in later outbreaks are usually not as bad as they are the first time.

Unlike gonorrhea or syphilis, genital herpes has no known cure. However, there are ways to relieve the symptoms. A drug called acyclovir can clear up painful sores and blisters. It can also help you have fewer and shorter outbreaks of genital herpes, although it cannot cure you. To get acyclovir, you need a prescription from a doctor.

If you think you may have herpes, see a doctor while you still have symptoms. The doctor will look at the area, take a sample from the sores, and test it to see if the herpes virus is present. The test will not work if the sores have healed, and it might not even work if they are more than a few days old. So act quickly.

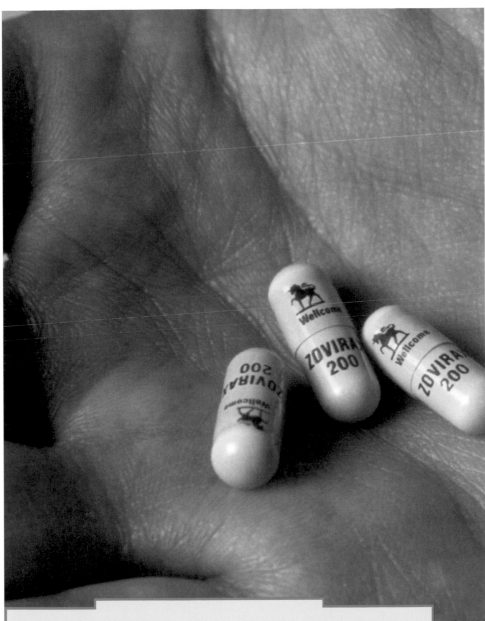

Certain types of herpes can often be treated with antiviral drugs such as Zovirax (acyclovir). Zovirax slows the growth and spread of the virus to allow the body's resources to fight off infection.

It is normal to feel panicked or depressed when you find out you have herpes. Do not be afraid to talk to others about your feelings. In fact, doctors recommend finding emotional support because herpes is aggravated by stress. Since herpes outbreaks can be triggered by stress as well as illness, it is important to eat properly, stay healthy, and learn how to manage stress.

The Facts About Genital Warts and Human Papillomavirus (HPV)

Genital warts are now the fastest-growing STD, according to a report by the Kaiser Family Foundation. Genital warts are a common STD. This disease affects an estimated twenty-four million Americans, with women younger than the age of twenty-five being the most highly infected group. In fact, it is thought that 30 to 40 percent of women in this age group actually have genital warts. Genital warts are caused by a group of viruses called HPV (human papillomavirus) that live inside skin cells. There are seventy different kinds of HPV. Not all of them cause genital warts. Certain kinds of HPV can also cause cancer. Some people with HPV do not know they have it. HPV is spread by direct skin-to-skin contact with someone who has the infection, usually through vaginal, anal, or oral sex.

Genital warts are growths or bumps that appear on parts of the body used during sex: the penis, vulva, and vagina, and even the thigh or throat. Often they are in hard-to-spot places, like inside the vagina or on the cervix or the anus. They may be skin-colored, small or large, bumpy or flat, and painless.

They may show up alone or in groups, and some may look like cauliflower. If you notice any unusual growths, bumps, or skin changes around your genitals, seek medical treatment immediately. Genital warts can multiply and spread very quickly. The longer they grow, the harder it is to get rid of them. Tell your doctor if you have any unusual itching, pain, or bleeding. When detected, the warts can be removed through medication or surgery. With treatment, the virus can be controlled. For women, getting regular Pap smears is important in diagnosing HPV.

The virus, however, can stay in the body for a long time and can cause future outbreaks. There are also cases in which people do not know they have HPV because the virus causes no symptoms. People can unknowingly infect others and transmit the virus easily. In women HPV is the major cause of cervical cancer. It has been reported that a condom does not provide total protection during sex because it does not prevent contact with pubic skin. If you are able to see the warts in the genital area, sexual contact should be avoided. The safest way to not contract genital warts and HPV is by not having sex at all. If you find out that you have genital warts, tell your sex partners. They may have the virus, too.

How to Prevent STDs

Contracting a sexually transmitted disease is a serious matter. You have already read about some of the different types of STDs and how they can affect your health and your life. You are less

Often, the best way to prevent contracting an STD is simply by communicating. Talk with your parents about any questions you may have regarding STDs or sexuality in general.

likely to contract an STD if you educate yourself about the risks of having sex.

Your teenage years are a time of great change, which often brings a good deal of confusion. Your body will undergo drastic changes and so will your emotions. This is a normal process of establishing your identity. As you establish your identity, you will become interested in things that you have not heard of or tried before—some good, some bad.

Talking to your parents about sex can clear up some of your problems. Some teens feel awkward discussing sex with their parents, perhaps because they are embarrassed or afraid of upsetting them. A counselor or doctor may offer more objective advice. If you are confused, worried, or suspect that you may have an STD, then always seek help immediately.

It is important to take your time and think carefully about having sex and the possible consequences, such as STDs. It is also your responsibility to take care of yourself and make sure that you practice safe sex.

Let's review some important factors when having sex: Always use a condom (especially with spermicide) during sex. Know your partner's sexual history. A monogamous relationship with an uninfected sex partner is safer. Examine your body regularly, and if you notice anything unusual, visit a doctor as soon as possible. Leaving an STD untreated will create more, possibly long-term, complications. Remember that you can greatly reduce the risk of contracting STDs by prevention. Prevention will save you a lot of time, money, and discomfort. As the old saying goes, an ounce of prevention is worth a pound of cure.

Glossary

AIDS Acquired immunodeficiency syndrome, a sexually transmitted disease.

blood transfusion Putting one person's blood into another person.

cervix The opening of the uterus.

condom A contraceptive; a rubber casing that is placed over the erect penis. The female condom is placed into the vagina.

contagious Transmitted from one person to another.

cytomegalovirus A type of herpes virus passed to newborn babies by the mother.

fallopian tubes Tubes that carry eggs from the ovaries to the uterus.

fatigue Tiredness.

fertilize To inseminate an egg and start a life.

genital herpes A sexually transmitted disease caused by the herpes simplex virus.

genital warts A sexually transmitted disease caused by the human papillomavirus.

gonorrhea A sexually transmitted disease caused by bacteria.

homosexual Describes a person who is attracted to or has sexual feelings for someone of the same sex.

human immunodeficiency virus (HIV) The virus that causes AIDS.

human papillomavirus (HPV) A group of viruses that live inside skin cells and cause genital warts.

immune system The system that fights infection in the body.

incubation Growth time.

infectious Contagious; able to be passed from one person to another.

latent Hidden.

menstruation Monthly female bleeding; also referred to as a period.

mucous membrane The soft lining inside organs such as the mouth, vagina, and rectum.

ovaries The organs that contain the eggs in a female.

Pap smear A method for the early detection of cancer cells in the female genital tract.

paralysis An inability to move.

pelvic inflammatory disease (PID) An infection of the female reproductive system.

penis The male external sex organ.

pus A white liquid that collects in sores and infected areas.

safe sex Sexual activity using contraceptives, such as condoms, to prevent transmitting STDs.

scrotum The sac that holds the testes (testicles).

semen The liquid from the penis that contains sperm.

sexual intercourse The joining of sexual organs, usually involving the ejaculation of semen; copulation.

sperm Male fertilizing organisms.

spirochete The germ that causes syphilis.

STD (sexually transmitted disease) Any disease that is transmitted through sexual contact.

syphilis A sexually transmitted disease caused by spirochetes.

testicles The testes; glands that produce sperm in the male.

tumors Bumps or lumps of tissue that form in the body.

urethra The tube that carries urine from the bladder; in the male, it also carries sperm through the penis.

uterus Womb; the sac in which the fetus develops.

vagina The place in a woman's body that leads from the uterus to the outside of the body.

venereal disease A sexually transmitted disease.

virus An organism that invades the cells of the body.

The Alan Guttmacher Institute
120 Wall Street, 21st Floor
New York, NY 10005
(800) 355-0244
Web site: http://www.guttmacher.org
The Guttmacher Institute's mission is to protect the reproductive choices of all women and men and support their
ability to obtain the information and services needed to
achieve their full human rights, safeguard their health,
and exercise their individual responsibilities in regard to
sexual behavior and relationships, reproduction, and
family formation.

The American Social Health Association (ASHA)
P.O. Box 13827
Research Triangle Park, NC 27713
(919) 361-8400
(800) 230-6039
Web site: http://www.ashastd.org
Confidential brochures on HPV, information on local support groups, and an online HPV chatroom are available
from ASHA. To obtain brochures call (800) 230-6039.
ASHA will also answer questions about HPV through e-
mail, at hpvnet@ashastd.org.

Canadian Federation for Sexual Health
1 Nicholas Street, Suite 430
Ottawa, ON K1N 7B7
Canada
(613) 241-4474
Web site: http://www.cfsh.ca
This charitable organization is dedicated to promoting
sexual and reproductive health and rights in Canada and
internationally.

Centers for Disease Control and Prevention (CDC)
National STD Hotline
1600 Clifton Road
Atlanta, GA 30333
(800) 227-8922
Web site: http://www.cdc.gov
Information to address your health concerns, as well as scien-
tific information on infectious diseases, is available through
the Web site of the CDC. They also offer educational and
student resources for grades K–12. The Web site features an
easy-to-use index of infectious diseases, including sexually
transmitted diseases.

National Women's Health Network
514 10th Street NW, Suite 400
Washington, DC 20005
(202) 347-1140
Web site: http://www.nwhn.org

The National Women's Health Network seeks to improve the
health of all women by developing and promoting a critical
analysis of health issues in order to affect policy and support consumer decision making.

Society of Obstetricians and Gynaecologists of Canada (SOGC)
780 Echo Drive
Ottawa, ON K1S 5R7
Canada
(613) 730-4192
Web site: http://www.sogc.org
The SOGC is a national medical society representing over
three thousand obstetricians/gynaecologists, family physi-
cians, nurses, midwives, and allied health professionals in
the field of sexual reproductive health.

Web Sites

Due to the changing nature of Internet links, Rosen Publishing
has developed an online list of Web sites related to the subject
of this book. This site is updated regularly. Please use this link
to access the list:

http://www.rosenlinks.com/faq/stds

Bronwen, Pardes. *Doing It Right: Making Smart, Safe, and Satisfying Choices About Sex*. New York, NY: Simon & Schuster, 2007.

Brynie, Faith Hickman. *101 Questions About Sex and Sexuality... with Answers for the Curious, Cautious, and Confused*. Fairfield, IA: Twenty-First Century Books, 2003.

Haerens, Margaret, ed. *Sexually Transmitted Diseases*. Detroit, MI: Greenhaven Press, 2007.

Haffner, Debra W. *Beyond the Big Talk: Every Parent's Guide to Raising Sexually Healthy Teens from Middle School to High School and Beyond*. New York, NY: Newmarket Press. 2002.

Hyde, Margaret, and Elizabeth Forsyth. *Safe Sex 101: An Overview for Teens*. New York, NY: Twenty-First Century Books, 2006.

Kolesnikow, Tassia. *Sexually Transmitted Diseases*. San Diego, CA: Lucent Books, 2004.

Kollar, Linda, and Brian R. Shmaefsky. *Gonorrhea* (Deadly Diseases and Epidemics). New York, NY: Chelsea House, 2005.

Libby, Roger W. *The Naked Truth About Sex: A Guide to Intelligent Sexual Choices for Teenagers and Twentysomethings*. Topanga, CA: Freedom Press, 2006.

Luadzers, Darcy. *Virgin Sex for Boys: A No-Regrets Guide for Safe and Healthy Sex*. Long Island City, NY: Hatherleigh Press, 2006.

Nardo, Don. *Human Papillomavirus (HPV)* (Diseases and Disorders). Farmington Hills, MI: Lucent Books, 2007.

Silverstein, Alvin, Virginia Silverstein, and Laura Silverstein Nunn. *The STDs Update* (Disease Update). Berkeley Heights, NJ: Enslow Publishers, 2006.

Spencer, Juliet V. *Cervical Cancer* (Deadly Diseases and Epidemics). New York, NY: Chelsea House, 2007.

Index

About the Authors

Nicholas Collins is a writer living in New Jersey, and Samuel G. Woods is a writer living in Chicago.

Photo Credits

Cover © www.istockphoto.com/Tracy Whiteside; p. 5 Ron Levine/Riser/Getty Images; pp. 7, 15, 16, 24–25, 39 Shutterstock; p. 9 Goodshoot/Jupiterimages/Thinkstock; p. 13 David Phillips/Visuals Unlimited; p. 22 David M. Phillips/Photo Researchers; p. 27 BSIP/Photo Researchers; p. 33 Michael Abbey/Visuals Unlimited; p. 34 Martin M. Rotker/Photo Researchers; p. 37 Dr. David Phillips/Visuals Unlimited/Getty Images; p. 42 iStockphoto/Thinkstock; p. 46 Beckman/Custom Medical Stock Photo; p. 49 Southern Illinois University/Photo Researchers; p. 52 Comstock/Thinkstock.

Designer: Evelyn Horovicz; Editor: Nick Croce; Photo Researcher: Marty Levick